Descendants of Jaquelin Ambler.

Genealogy of the descendants of my grandfather, JAQUELIN AMBLER, and REBECCA, daughter of LEWIS BURWELL, of Gloucester, extracted from the old family Bible which my parents used up to the time of my father's death, on the 25th March, 1857, the same being written in a strong, bold hand on the leaf commencing with the New Testament Scriptures, as follows:

Jaquelin Ambler (son of Richard Ambler) born 9th August, 1742, married Rebecca (daughter of Lewis Burwell, of Gloucester) 24th May, 1764, her age being 18, and had issue as follows:

Elizabeth Jaquelin Ambler, born 11th March, 1765. *Obit* Feb. 15th, 1842.

Mary Willis Ambler. born 18th March, 1766. *Obit* December 26th, 1831.

Martha Burwell Ambler, born 23d Nov., 1767. *Obit* 11th July, 1773.

Rebecca Ambler, born 1st December, 1769. *Obit* 11th December, 1769.

Rebecca Nelson Ambler, born 22d Jan., 1771. *Obit* 17th April, 1772.

Ann Ambler, born 16th Nov., 1772. *Obit* 28th June, 1832.

John Ambler, born 23d Jan., 1775. *Obit* 19th June following.

Lucy Nelson Ambler, born 4th August, 1776, at New Castle, Hanover county, and died in Richmond 27th April, 1846.

(Then follows the following, written by my mother. The dates of death were written on and after 1831 by some one of her children.—G. D. F.)

" I will show mercy unto a thousand generations of them that love me and keep my commandments,"—let this be remembered now in the fifth generation.

> "We boast not that we derive our birth
> From loins enthroned, or valors of the earth ;
> But higher far our proud pretensions rise ;
> Children of parents passed into the skies."

The above children of Jaquelin Ambler and Rebecca Burwell married as follows :

Elizabeth Jaquelin married her first husband, William Brent, Esq., who soon died ; married her second husband Col. Edward Carrington, and died without issue 15th Feb., 1842.

Mary Willis married John Marshall, Esq., afterwards Chief-Justice of the United States, and had six children, who married as follows :

Thomas married Miss Margaret Lewis, of Wyanoke in Charles City county, Va., and afterwards settled at "Oak Hill" in the county of Fauquier. Thomas Marshall was a man of talent. He represented his county often in the Legislature, and was a member of the Convention of 1829, which gave a new Constitution to Virginia.

Jaquelin Ambler, who married Miss Clarkson, of Fauquier. and settled in that county. He studied medicine, and was called Dr., but did not practice outside of his own family.

Mary, who married General Jaquelin Burwell Harvie, settled in Richmond. He entered the navy as midshipman, and rose to be lieutenant. He then resigned. Shortly after his marriage he represented first the city of Richmond, then the county of Henrico in the House of Delegates, and afterwards the district in the Senate.

John married Miss Alexander, of Baltimore, and settled in the county of Fauquier, which he represented in the House of Delegates.

James Keith married Claudia Burwell, of Gloucester county, Va., and settled in the county of Fauquier.

Edward Carrington married Rebecca Peyton, of Gloucester county, Va., and also settled in the county of Fauquier. The Chief-Justice, their father, gave them all handsome estates in the manor of Leeds, in the same neighborhood.

The following is a list of the *grandchildren* of Chief-Justice John Marshall and Mary Willis Ambler—

(Thomas, the eldest son, had eight children, viz :)

John, married Miss Blackwell.
Agnes, married Alex. G. Taliaferro.
Mary, married Wm. B. Archer.
Fielding Lewis, married 1st Rebecca Coke ; 2d wife, Miss
    Thomas.
Ann Lewis, married James F. Jones.
Margaret Lewis, married John Thomas Smith.
Thomas, married Miss Barton.

(Jaquelin, the second son, had seven children, viz :)

Mary Ambler, married Robert Douthat.
Mildred Pickett, unmarried.
Eliza Clarkson, married Harrison Robertson.
Ann Maria, married Elliott Braxton.
Jaquelin Ambler, married 1st Miss Sherrard, and his second
    wife was Rebecca Marshall.
Wm. Clarkson, married Kate Edloe.
Ellen Harvie, married Charles M. Barton.

(Mary, the third child, had nine children, viz :)

Mary Marshall, unmarried.
John Marshall, unmarried.
Ellen Strother, married Frank G. Ruffin.
Virginia, married Dr. Spicer Patrick.
Susan Colston, married Rev. Anderson Wade.
William Wallace, unmarried.
Ann Fisher, unmarried.
Lewis, unmarried.
Emily, unmarried.

(John, the fourth child, had four children, viz :)

John, unmarried.
Ashton Alexander, unmarried.
James Edward, married Mary Morris Marshall.
Mary Willis, married Fielding L. Douthat.

(James Keith, the fifth child, had twelve children, viz :)

John, married Mildred Stribling.
Nath'l Burwell, married Sally Ewing.

James Keith, married Fanny Ambler.
Maria Willis, unmarried.
Mary Ambler, married Lewis Coleman.
Ann Burwell, married Rev. Geo. H. Norton.
Thomas, unmarried.
Alice Lewis, married Gray Carroll.
Claudia Hamilton, married Hilary P. Jones.
Edward Carrington, married Bell Raeney.
Eliza Jaquelin, unmarried.
Rebecca Peyton, married Henry Stribling.

(Edward, the sixth child, had eight children, viz :)

John, married 1st Lou Fitzhugh ; 2d wife, Willie Jones.
Mary Lewis, unmarried.
Rebecca Peyton, married Jaquelin Marshall.
Edward Carrington, married Virginia Taylor.
James Keith, unmarried and killed in battle.
Betsy Lewis, married Willoughby Newton.
Jaquelin Ambler, married Mary Douthat.
Courtney, married Thomas Marshall.

Ann Ambler, the sixth child of Jaquelin Ambler and Rebecca
Burwell, married George Fisher at Gielston the 29th May, 1795,
and had issue as follows. (Gielston was a part of the 40 acres
commonly known as " Buchanan's Spring," and now at the head
of Broad street, on a lower part of which the new brick depot of
the R., F. & P. R. R. is built.)

Mary Rebecca Fisher, born 29th March, 1796. *Obit* 15th June,
1796.
John Alex. Buchanan Fisher, born 11th May, 1797. *Obit* 28th
October, 1815.
Elizabeth Jaquelin Fisher, born 28th Dec., 1798. *Obit* 17th Au-
gust, 1845.
Jaquelin Ambler Fisher, born 28th October, 1800. *Obit* 20th
July, 1803.
Jane Ravenscroft Fisher, born 27th July, 1802. *Obit* 18th April,
1886.
George Daniel Fisher, born 11th December, 1804.
Lucy Marshall Fisher, born 10th March, 1807. *Obit* 22d Sep-
tember, 1874.

Edward Carrington Fisher, born 16th November, 1809.   *Obit* 12th January, 1890.

Mary Ann Ambler Fisher, born 1st June, 1811.   *Obit* 27th August, 1863.

Charles Fenton Mercer Fisher, born 22d December, 1813.   *Obit* 17th September, 1848.

Mrs. Ann Fisher, mother of the above ten children, died on the 28th of June, 1832, at the old family residence of her father, on 10th between Marshall and Clay streets, and was interred in Shockoe Hill cemetery in the same section with her husband, Mr. George Fisher, who died at the same residence 25th March, 1857.

The children of Ann Ambler and George Fisher married as follows:

Elizabeth Jaquelin married Mr. Thomas Marshall Colston, of the county of Loudoun, Va., and was interred in Trinity churchyard at Staunton.

Jane Ravenscroft married Mr. Carter H. Harrison, of Cumberland county, Va., and was interred in the cemetery at Fredericksburg, Va.

George Daniel married 1st Elizabeth Garrigues Higginbotham, of Albemarle county, and 2d E. Harriet Haxall, of Richmond, Va.

Lucy Marshall married, as the 2d wife, Daniel Norbourn Norton, and was interred in Hollywood cemetery, Richmond, Va.

Edward Carrington married Lavinia Page, and was interred in Hollywood cemetery.

Mary Ann Ambler married, as the second wife, Nicholas C. Kinney, of Staunton, Va., and was interred in Trinity churchyard, Staunton, Va.

Charles Fenton Mercer married Mary Eskridge, of Mississippi, and was interred in Shockoe Hill cemetery, Richmond, Va.

The following is a list of the *grandchildren* of Ann Ambler and George Fisher.

(Elizabeth Jaquelin had three children, viz:)

Raleigh married Gertrude Powell, of Loudon county.

Ann F, married Professor John B. Minor.

Susan married Charles M. Blackford.

(Jane Ravenscroft had six children, viz :)

> *George Fisher Harrison*, married 1st Sally Brown ; 2d, Rebecca Conrad; 3d, Susan M. Royall, and 4th, Eula Holman.
>
> *Jaquelin*, married 1st Betty Conrad; 2d, Betty Powell, and 3d, Susan Ficklin.
>
> *Carter*, married Alice Williams.
>
> *Henry*, married Jane Cochran.
>
> *Betty Ambler*, married Wm. H. Fitzhugh.
>
> *Mary Ann*, married Wm. H. Fitzhugh as his 2d wife.

(George Daniel had four children, viz :)

> *Mary Elmslie*, married Peyton Randolph.
>
> *Ann*, married George W. Camp, of Norfolk, Va.
>
> *Robert Haxall*, married Eleanor Heth Taylor, of Staunton, Va.
>
> *Edward Higginbotham*, married 1st Marrabella Sherman Taylor, of Staunton, Va.; 2d, Eliza Leroy Daingerfield, of Augusta, county, Va.

(Lucy Marshall had five children, viz :)

> *John Hatley*, married Mrs. Louisa Leach.
>
> *George Fisher*, unmarried.
>
> *Nannie*, unmarried.
>
> *Norborn*, married Mary Mahoney.
>
> *Elizabeth*, unmarried.

(Edward Carrington had six children, viz :)

> *George*, married Agnes Woodfin.
>
> *John Page*, unmarried.
>
> *Edward Carrington*, unmarried.
>
> *Nannie*, married Wm. H. Kennon.
>
> *Eliza Page*, unmarried.
>
> *Charles*, married Maria Ramsay Jervey, of S. C.

(Mary Ann had three children, viz :)

> *Alexander F.*, married Virginia Galt, of Fluvanna Co.
>
> *John Marshall*, married Mary Beirne, of Monroe Co.
>
> *Edward Carrington*, unmarried.

Lucy Nelson Ambler, the eighth child of Jaquelin Ambler and

Rebecca Burwell, married Daniel Call and had one daughter, who married Daniel N. Norton, and died in childbirth *with* her infant.

———

The record just finished of the descendants of Jaquelin Ambler and Rebecca Burwell down to the *third* generation, is increased in interest by a recital of the noble and valuable character drawn by Mrs. Carrington, his eldest daughter, in one of her letters to her sister, Mrs. Ann Fisher, of their father, and also by the Rev. John Buchanan, who resided for some years in Mr. Ambler's family, and preached his funeral sermon. In order to produce a like interest by the descendants in this recital, I have introduced Mrs. Carrington's letter following the genealogy, and also the sermon of Mr. Buchanan. Thus—

To Mrs. ANN FISHER:

Dear Nancy,—In my first letter I dwelt entirely upon the virtues of our estimable mother; now would I bring the best of fathers to your recollection. His saint-like image is too deeply impressed to need any picture of mine to recall him to your remembrance. I find a complete portrait of him drawn by the inimitable Cowper at the conclusion of his "Winter Walk at Noon," beginning, "He is the happy man whose life even now shows somewhat of a happier life to come"; every line throughout portrays the character of our much loved father so completely that I could wish, if it were possible, that all his descendants like myself would commit it to memory, and also that the character given him at his death by Mr. R. and Mr. Buchanan, which you have in the sermon, may be preserved; also a letter to Miss Caines. Your children, at some future time, will dwell with delight on having such ancestors, and may repeat with Cowper—

> "We boast not that we derive our birth
> From loins enthroned or rulers of the earth;
> But higher far our proud pretensions rise;
> Children of parents passed into the skies."

A distinguished piety, as I have learned from our venerable aunt, marked the character of our father from earliest youth. No doubt this had great weight in the selection he made of our mother. Never in this particular were minds more congenial, and for upwards of thirty years they lived in the constant reciprocation of connubial affection. This was a source of great comfort to themselves, and of never ceasing advantage to their children, who under every circumstance have felt the advantage of their example. Our poor mother being too infirm to engage much in the care of her children, it almost entirely devolved on our father; and when my sister, Marshall, and myself were barely five and six years old, he went through the arduous task of teaching us, and in every particular supplying the place of a mother, notwithstanding he held an office (collector of the King's customs at York) that afforded little leisure for such employment. The moment he left his chamber in the morning, which was at an early hour, we were called, and throughout the day every hour from business was devoted to us. Our copies, as soon as we could write, were written in the fairest hand by himself, short, but always containing a lesson of piety or an elegant moral quotation; the orthography and grammar entirely defective, which we were to correct. No English grammar at that time was to be found. Parents and teachers in later times owe much to Lindley Murray in that branch of education, but in my own opinion the good old-fashioned *teaching* to *spell* has greatly the advantage over the modern. Our arithmetic commenced most pleasantly. The first figures, I well remember, were encircled with flowers, which had a happy effect in drawing our attention.

Amusing books were carelessly left open on the writing table; letters from the children of his friends in Philadelphia were given us to answer, and our education went on without rule or forms. Had it been our lot to come into life a little later, much trouble might have been spared by the after-publications of a Baubauld, an Edgeworth, etc. The " Preceptor," a large volume, differing from any other I have ever seen, was imported by my father, and was really a valuable work, comprising lessons of various sorts, interspersed with pleasant stories, and some well selected poetry. Thus did our dear father devote himself to us, and pursue every means in his power to give us instruction, at a time when girls in our country were simply taught to read and write at £25 and a load of wood per year. A boarding-school was nowhere in Virginia to be found. Such attentions as we experienced were without a parallel ; it was thought, however, to have too much of

severity, for the rod at that time was an implement never to be dis·
pensed with, and our dear father used it most conscientiously.
By many he was considered a most rigid disciplinarian, but I
have since discovered that his superior knowledge of human
nature led him to pursue the right course, and in my own subsequent experience in the education of children, I have found
that the present prevailing opinion that youth may be reared and
matured by indulgence, is altogether erroneous.   There are dis-
positions, and amongst those that I have had the direction of I
have had one perhaps that such a course may be pursued without
injury ; but I will venture to say, with a very few exceptions, it
will be always proper to observe a well regulated discipline.
Nothing is so well calculated to inspire youthful minds with
respect and confidence towards their parents and teachers.   Restraint is certainly never pleasant, and to children is insupport-
able, but it is productive of every good, in every situation, and
gives a zest to after enjoyment in life that nothing else can supply ;
that it forms the mind to bear its ills has never been denied.

The advantages I have experienced through life from my
father's supposed inflexibility are incalculable.   First, a remarkable thoughtless and giddy childishness rendered a constant
discipline on his part necessary, which produced that restraint
the good effects of which are felt to this day, and no doubt in
every situation, and particularly in one, the most important of my
life, prevented the most fatal consequences.   We often hear the
observation, and sometimes from parents that we are inclined
generally to think well of, that a rigid parent never has an
obedient child.   My own experience certainly disproves it.
When the parent is found to unite the character of the virtuous
Christian with the conscientious disciplinarian, he will never cease
to be loved and respected ; there is no sacrifice of inclination or
self-will that a child will not be induced to make to such a parent;
and who can describe the heartfelt delight we experience when
the time of restraint is passed, and the parent becomes the friend
instead of the master ; when we are capable of reflecting that
every restraint was imposed for our good ; that the infliction
cost him more pain than we felt, and that upon every occasion
his first and greatest concern was the good of his child.   Such
a father was ours, and the love and respect he inspired us with
has seldom been equalled.   Never shall I forget the impression

made on me when he first relaxed in what was termed his rigid conduct.   Certainly I should never have tasted half its pleasures had he been always in the habit of indulging.

As a great mark of favor I was permitted, at the age of fourteen, to accept an invitation of our Aunt A. in Hanover. Before I finished my journey I received a letter from him telling me he now considered I had arrived at an age when I might, in some degree, be left to myself. "Remember, my child,"—these were his words—"this is the first time you have left the wing of tender parents; it behooves you to be watchful over your conduct ; to be affable and courteous to all around you. Much depends upon your first entrance in the world; but, above all, never neglect your daily duty to your Great Benefactor. He demands your warmest gratitude."

This was the first time he ever called my attention to religious duties. No doubt he felt perfectly satisfied with what our mother did for us in this particular, but his own constant example was of itself sufficient and of far greater weight than precept. Never did man live in more constant practices of religious duties ; early and late we knew him in the performance of them. It was his daily habit to spend his first and latest hours in prayer and meditation. Every Sunday that his church was open he was the first to enter it, and often would be almost a solitary male at the table of God.

[At the time alluded to our country was thrown into great confusion by the long continuance of the war, and afterwards seemed to imbibe too much of that infidelity that so much prevailed when Paine and Godwin disseminated their writings abroad, and a more insinuating distinguished personage gave his lessons at home. The churches in Virginia were almost entirely shut up and their ordinances unobserved; most of our men engaged in the war.]

It is not remembered whether he considered days of fasting as necessary, but his frequent abstinence led us to believe that he felt the necessity of it, and perhaps his constitution also induced him often to practice it ; nevertheless, he was never religiously gloomy. His temper was not gay, but his seriousness was generally the effect of a continual devotion to business and a remarkably reflecting mind. However, there were seasons when he enjoyed society and would often use exertions to amuse his

young friends.   The company of children, when quiet and play-
ful, was delightful to him, and I have often known him seek it to
avoid those of larger growth; with them he used to say he
always found innocence.   Benevolence in its utmost extent
marked the character of our much loved father through every
period of his life, and the pecuniary sacrifices for it made by him
are beyond calculation.   His secret charities have often been
repeated in my ear from grateful lips that dared not, from delicacy for his feelings, repeat them abroad.

From her affectionate sister,

E. J. C.

There was living in Richmond a poor Scotch clergyman
named John Buchanan, whom he invited to make his house his
home until he should be able to support himself.   The invitation
was accepted.   The excellent Parson Buchanan lived with him
till he died, officiated when he was consigned to the grave, and
preached his funeral sermon, from which the following extract is
made :

And when can we more seasonably apply to these duties,
than when we are warned by the loss of our friends to remember our latter end, and "apply our hearts unto wisdom."   We
have, my brethren, been lately paying the last sad tribute to a
departed brother.   He whose loss we now lament had passed
the fifty-fifth year of his age without a blemish to his reputation,
without an enemy, with numerous friends.   Adored by his family,
he has almost consoled them for his loss by the conviction that
he has not gone too early for himself, and that he was mature in
character, notwithstanding the constant exposure of an official
man to the displeasure of others by the impartiality of his conduct.   Even those who went away from him unindulged in their
applications, were satisfied by a confidence in the purity of his
motives.

His public career for nearly twenty years was a series of testimony to this truth.   Drawn from the peaceful walks of private
life into public action, with but a solicitation or a wish previously
expressed, he was chosen by the Legislature to their important
offices during the Revolution and since the peace.   His last,
that of *Treasurer,* presented for thirteen years to malice, envy,

or enmity, had they existed against him, an annual opportunity
of gratification.   And yet was he annually re-elected, because he
had unremittingly shown his fitness for the office.   His fatal dis-
order put human nature on the rack, but he bore his agonies with
every firmness of which human nature was capable, cherished,
strengthened and animated by the divine glow of Christianity,
and foreseeing, with a smile, the prospect opening to his view.
The poor scarcely knew the hand from which they so often received relief.   And those who were his dependents could not
but own how much their condition was softened by the kindness
of their master.   To this fair transcript of his character, drawn
by one who knew him well, both in his public and private life,
I might, from a fourteen years' knowledge of him (ten whereof I
spent in his family), add many private traits which characterize
him as the good man and sincere, pious Christian.   I could set
before you innumerable instances of kind attention and anxious
solicitude to alleviate the distresses, bear the infirmities, provide
for the wants, nay even anticipate the wishes of her to whom he
was united.   Of the constant care and unremitted assiduity of the
fond but judicious parent, training up his own children, as also
the fatherless, and those who had none to guide and direct them
in the path of religion and virtue, not merely by daily precepts,
but by what is infinitely more efficacious, by daily example, conscientiously discharging that most important of all trusts, and
securing their temporal as well as eternal interests.   I might
bear honorable testimony to his being as tender of the reputation
of another, repelling every report circulated by envy or malice
against his neighbor's fame, and like Christian charity "thinking
no evil."   I might adduce repeated proofs of his delicacy and
purity of manners and conversation, and of his temperance and
self-government.

He may, however, have been thought by some too reserved and
too much of a recluse, and that he separated himself more than
was necessary from scenes of cheerful and innocent sociability.
But it may be truly said that none had greater enjoyment in his
family and the private circle of his friends, whenever the state of
his health would permit, and that he was sufficiently conversant
in the world to present to it a fair model of integrity and a constant attention to his duties as an officer, though not enough to
be seduced and contaminated by its follies and vices.   To sum

up all, I might lead you to his private retirement, and present to you the devout Christian, prostrate in humble supplication before his Almighty Creator, which they only who follow his example can justly estimate, and which they know proves their greatest consolation in the various trials and calamities of life.   In fine, I might conduct you to the altar of God, where you would hear him making a public profession of his faith, and, regardless of the scoffs of the infidel and the ridicule of a vain and inconsiderate world, giving an open and solemn testimony that he was not ashamed of the Cross of Christ, which was to him both the wisdom and power of God to his salvation.   These and many more features of his character I might exhibit to your view ; but though a minute and particular detail would still appear to myself as falling short of his merit, yet to those less acquainted with him than I was it might seem to be drawn by the flattering pencil of a friend.   I therefore forbear a further recital, and make one reflection naturally arising from the subject, that whenever the eye of man is disgusted and shocked by scenes of impiety, rapine, cruelty and bloodshed, let him cast it on such a fair and pleasing picture as the present, which does so much honor to human nature, and he will not fail to conclude that man, the prey of furious and malignant passions, resembles an infernal spirit ; but when actuated by the sacred dictates of religion and devoted virtue, he claims kindred with the angels in heaven. " Mark, therefore, the perfect man and behold the upright, for the end of that man is peace."

In the year 1818 the second John Ambler, who was then living in the city of Richmond, received from James City county an old christening vase, which had been given to the church at James Town nearly a century before by the wife and son of his ancestor, Edward Jaquelin, Esquire, of James Town, which sacred vessel was saved in the general wreck of church plate, sold under an act of the Virginia Assembly passed in ————. It had this inscription engraven upon it :

"Given by Martha, the wife of Edward Jaquelin, and Edward, their son, for the use of the church in James City."

The last died in Hackny and was interred in Shadwell churchyard, aged eighteen years, 1733-'4.

The following lines were written on reception of this vase by Mrs. Elizabeth Jaquelin Carrington :

1.

Dear sacred vase! do I indeed behold
  This holy relic of my Church and sire ?
Not basely barter'd and profanely sold,
  But pure and perfect, still preserved entire.

2.

No sordid act could change thy sacred use,
  No impious tongue condemn a gift so dear,
While cup and chalice felt the dire abuse
  That echoes loud in heaven's offended ear.

3.

But thou, most precious vase, remained the same,
  Still waiting to perform the donor's will;
And when to man thou giv'st the Christian's name,
  The Spirit grant and grace divine instill.

The following is engraved around the rim of the silver baptismal basin described on this sheet, viz : "After the church in James City was destroyed this basin was returned to Col. John Ambler, of Jamestown, as the representative of the donor, and by him was presented, in the year 1831, to the Monumental Church, city of Richmond, upon the condition that it should be retained in all time in its present shape for the use of the Church."

A mahogany case has been made for it of proper size, and the rector's family have it in safe-keeping for the use of the church. My mother pointed out to me, many years before her death, the spot in St. John's Church burying-ground in which my grandmother and grandfather Ambler were interred, but no tombstones were erected over them, and I believe at their request should not be done. But the ground is now all levelled and turfed over, so that I am unable to point out the spot she showed me not less than sixty years ago.

I append also two letters of Mrs. Carrington to her sister, Mrs. Fisher, in 1810, which I am sure readers of this pamphlet (which is intended for the descendants of Mrs. Ambler chiefly) will derive pleasure from, in her delineation of the character of

her brother-in-law, Chief-Justice Marshall, as well as her experience in early life of the difficulties attending female education.

G. D. F.

1810.

My Dear Nancy :

If anything can supply the place of early education, it is
being thrown into a society where the infant mind may be led to
observations that may tend to future improvement. I cannot
say that this was precisely our situation when left as we were at
Winchester. Our female relation was truly amiable, but young
and inexperienced, and almost as childish as ourselves. Her
husband, though a man of sterling worth, and one whom I still
love and venerate beyond most of my friends, was too much occupied or too negligent to bestow those attentions upon us that we
required. Thus was my sister, my cousin, a little older than
myself, and I (most of all unmanageable) were left entirely to our
own wayward humors, and but for the remarkable discretion
of my sister, who was only twelve years of age, my cousin and
myself would have been perpetually involved in difficulties. As
it was, the absurdities of my conduct can never be thought of
but with regret, nor would I, for any consideration, have our
Janetta, or any girl that I love, placed in a similar situation. A
girl of thirteen, left without an adviser, of a gay and frivolous
temper, fancying herself a woman, stands on a precipice that
trembles beneath her. The society of Winchester consisted of
all descriptions of persons who seek a new country to better
their fortunes ; thus you may suppose there could be little refine-
ment, and of course little improvement gained amongst them.
There were, however, a few genteel and respectable families,
English, Irish, and Dutch, but the chief population was Dutch.
During our stay we often met with genteel travellers, and not
unfrequently made acquaintance with agreeable men who were
condemned in various parts to banishment to this dreary place
on account of disaffection, as it was called, to the great cause of
liberty. In this remote corner they were entirely precluded any
intercourse with Britain or British agents ; of course unable, if
they had the disposition, to enter into any plans with them.
Amongst those proscribed, genteel Quakers from Philadelphia
were numerous, and I also remember with much affection a

Colonel Elligood, from Norfolk.   Added to these there were many charming young officers who had been prisoners in Canada, and just then liberated; such were Heth, Bruin, McGuire, etc., etc. Here was a fine field open for a romantic girl to exhibit in, and here I could tell you many pretty stories of sighing swains, tender billets, love-inspiring sonnets, etc., etc., but that they would be blended with so many childish absurdities that I will not venture to repeat them.   Fortunately, nature blessed me with that versatility of temper that at that time it would have been impossible to have fixed my attention to any one object, so that, consequently, I escaped an entanglement that might have eventuated in regret.   Early in the spring our good father returned and withdrew us from scenes that were so truly improper, and though he treated us himself as children, yet it was evident he saw that we had been considered of an age to attract too much attention.   The only consolation I have ever felt for these youthful follies was that, in a subsequent visit to Winchester, I found that my temper and deportment, to those of my acquaintances who remained there, had been such as to inspire them with an affection for me which had induced them to throw a veil over my youthful follies, and that they continued to love me with unabated affection.

It is not a pleasant thing to retrace the follies of youth, but I have determined, by a candid representation of different periods of my life, to guard our dear little girl against errors that I have fallen into.   If our lives are prolonged probably she may not be exposed or placed in similar situations, and now certain it is that another Revolutionary war can never happen to affect and ruin a family so completely as ours has been.   The only possible good from the entire change in our circumstances was, that we were made acquainted with the manners and situation of our own country, which we otherwise should never have known; added to this, necessity taught us to use exertions which our girls of the present day know nothing of.   We were forced to industry to appear genteelly, to study manners to supply the place of education, and to endeavor, by amiable and agreeable conduct, to make amends for the loss of fortune, which by this time was reduced to a pretty low ebb.   See us at this period reduced to the necessity of travelling in a common wagon, which to be sure was fixed comfortably with swinging seats, etc.; like the good old vicar's family, we were rather ashamed of our cavalry, but the constant attentions we received from all who knew the virtues and independent spirit of my father rendered our change more supportable.

One little mortification I must, however, relate : We arrived at Fredericksburg rather at a late hour in the evening ; our equipage was safely lodged; we passed the next day with our friends there ; had much attention paid us ; were invited to a ball in the evening that we declined going to, not having ball dresses with us (which by the by were not to be found elsewhere), and besides we were to take our departure at a very early hour in the morning, having prevailed on our father to let us walk to the skirts of the town where our vehicle would be in readiness for us.   When lo, and behold ! just as we were stepping into it, several genteel and elegant officers appeared, who had encamped with their regiment the preceding night at this very spot.   Here was a terrible blow to our fancied consequence; like the Miss Primroses, we began to bridle and perhaps would have glanced at better days and talked of the coach we had lately passed that way in on our journey up, but our vicar-like father cut the matter short by shaking hands with the gentlemen, all of whom he had known before, said he was carrying his children (for he still treated us as such) to join their mother, and wished them a good journey.   The commanding officer proved to be Colonel Carrington, afterwards the friend of all others most respected, and ultimately the husband of my choice.

Yours sincerely,   E. J. C.

My Dear Nancy :

Had I talents or the necessary information for writing the history of my country, the period of my life mentioned in my last would afford an ample opportunity to distinguish myself; but possessing neither the one nor the other, it is impossible to give you an idea of the interesting state of the colonies at that time—that eventful war, which I so often had occasion to dwell on, was at that period carried on in the northern States with the utmost vigor ; our own, however, for some time was exempt from its ravages, and we returned to our dear York—not, indeed, to our former mansion, but to a small retired tenement that had long been occupied by others. My imagination frequently recurs to the enchanting spot, situated on a little eminence in the environs of the town overlooking a smiling meadow where a gentle stream, meandering round the sloping hill, was lost in one of the noblest rivers in our country./ Here my sister and myself often wandered, gathering wild flowers to adorn our hair, till we almost fancied ourselves heroines. The charm, however, only lasted during our rambles, for on returning to the house we always found employment sufficient to convince us that much of the comfort of the family depended upon our personal exertions. My father at this time accepted an appointment which kept him almost constantly at Williamsburg. Our own town had now become a garrison; of course we should have been left to experience repeated alarms had we not been fortunately next door neighbor to the commanding officer, Colonel Marshall, with his *suite*, composed of several of his young relations, one of whom was often our immediate guard. It was at this time we became acquainted with our much loved brother, then called Captain Marshall, who, being without a command just then, left the northern army to visit his father and friends. Perhaps no officer that had been introduced to us excited so much interest. We had been accustomed to hear him spoken of by all as a very paragon. We had often seen letters from him fraught with filial and fraternal affection; the eldest of fifteen children, devoted from his earliest years to his younger brothers and sisters, he was almost idolized by them, and every line received from him was read with rapture. Our expectations were raised to the highest pitch, and the little circle of York was on tiptoe on his arrival. Our girls were particularly emulous who should be first introduced. It is remarkable that my sister, then only fourteen and diffident beyond all others, declared that we were giving ourselves useless trouble, for that she, for the first time, had made up her mind to go to the ball, though she had not even ever been at dancing school, and was resolved to set her cap at him and eclipse us all.

This in the end proved true, and at the first introduction he became devoted to her. For my own part I am free to confess that I felt not the slightest wish to contest the prize with her. In this, as in every other instance of life, my sister's superior discernment and solidity of character has made me feel my own insignificance. She with a glance developed his character, and understood how to appreciate it, while I, expecting an Adonis, lost all desire of becoming agreeable in his eyes when I beheld his awkward figure, unpolished manners, and total negligence of person (which by-the-by did often produce a blush on her cheek). Nevertheless how trivial now seem such objections. Under the slouched hat there beamed an eye that penetrated at one glance the inmost recesses of the human character, and beneath the slovenly garb there dwelt a heart replete with every virtue. What his superior mind and knowledge are capable of exhibiting, belongs to a more able biographer than myself; it is only his domestic character that I have attempted feebly to sketch. None ever knew him in that particular better than myself. From the moment he loved my sister he became truly a brother to me (a blessing which before I had never known,) and the reciprocal interest which we have each felt for the other has never known abatement. During the short stay he made with us, our whole family became attached to him, and though there was then no certainty of his becoming allied to us, we felt a love for him that can never cease. And how could it have been otherwise when there was no circumstance, however trivial, in which we were concerned, that was not his care. Much, indeed, do I owe him in every respect, and if I claim any consequence in life, it may be ascribed to my early intimacy with so estimable a friend. Certain it is, whatever taste I may have for reading was entirely gained from him, who used to read to *us* from the best authors, particularly the poets, with so much taste and pathos as to give me an idea of their sublimity, without which *I* should never have had an idea of. Thus did he lose no opportunity of blending improvement with our amusements, and thereby gave us a taste for books which probably we might never otherwise have had.

Soon after this we learned with pleasure that he was determined to attend the law studies in Williamsburg during his absence from his regiment of about three months, and at the end of that time, after obtaining a license, he rejoined his regiment, gaining as much in that short time as would have employed many the same number of years. On our way to Richmond, where we had been induced to remove in consequence of my father's appointment to council, when the government was removed to that place, we had the pleasure of seeing him in Williamsburg—we found him still the kind, attentive friend as in York. · Notwithstanding his amiable and correct conduct, there were those who would catch at the most trifling circumstances to throw a shade over his fair fame. Once in particular I remember an observation of one of his envious contemporaries, when allusion was made to his short stay at William and Mary College, that he could have gained but little there, and that his talents were greatly overrated. How far he has left this *wise observer* behind him, might be easily shown were I at liberty to describe the *distinguished personage.* The same spirit of envy and detraction has followed him more or less through life, and though no man living ever had more ardent friends; yet there does not exist one who had at one time more slandering enemies.

One remarkable trait, however, in his character is, that he was never known to make, even to his most intimate friend, an invidious or malevolent retort, though slanders were propagated and whispered in the ear of those with whom of all others he wished to stand well, insidiously representing the most trifling failings into crimes of blackest dye. Yet has he always preserved the same amiable, unsuspicious temper which so remarkably distinguishes him, and has wisely shown that nothing can so completely blunt the shaft of envy and malice as a life spent in virtuous and noble usefulness.

The year after the war his marriage took place at the cottage in Hanover, to which place we had been invited by our relation, John Ambler. It has been ill-naturedly said that my father made objections on the score of fortune, but nothing was ever less true, for though I have heard Mr. Marshall a hundred times declare that after paying the parson he had but one solitary guinea left, yet, had that been lacking, my father would have considered him the very best choice his daughter could have made; certainly the event has proved so, for no man in my estimation has ever, save one, stood so high in our country. What his conduct has been in the tender relations of domestic life, you have had as good an opportunity of knowing as myself—his exemplary tenderness to our unfortunate sister is without parallel; with a delicacy of frame and feeling that baffles all description, she became, early after her marriage, a prey to extreme nervous affection, which more or less has embittered her comfort through life, but this has only served to increase his care and tenderness,

and he is, as you well know, as entirely devoted as at the moment
of their first being married. Always and under every circumstance an enthusiast in love, I have very lately heard him declare that he looked with astonishment at the present race of
lovers, so totally unlike what he had been himself. His never-
failing cheerfulness and good-humor is a perpetual source of
delight to all connected with him, and I have not a doubt has
been the means of prolonging the life of her he is so tenderly
devoted to.

Instead of wearying you with my own trifling concerns and an
account of my unimportant life, I will occasionally give you a
sketch of characters who have been interesting to me, but for
the present will transcribe letters of old friends and select some
of my own that may serve to amuse you on rainy days.

Yours,   E. J. C.

ALDERMAN LIBRARY

The return of this book is due on the date
indicated below

DUE	DUE
MAR 3 0 1955	
1-25-89	
10/12/95	
1/15/96	
2·15·96